The Challenger Space
Shuttle Explosion

CODE RED

JANUARY 28, 1986

The Challenger Space Shuttle Explosion

by **William Caper**

Consultant: Michelle Nichols, Master Educator
Adler Planetarium & Astronomy Museum
Chicago, Illinois

BEARPORT
PUBLISHING

New York, New York

Credits

Cover and Title Page, © Corbis; 4, © Bettmann/CORBIS; 5, © AP Images/Bruce Weaver; 6, NASA Johnson Space Center (NASA-JSC); 7, NASA Johnson Space Center (NASA-JSC); 8, NASA Johnson Space Center (NASA-JSC); 9, © Bettmann/Corbis; 10TL, © Michael S. Yamashita/Corbis; 10BL, NASA Johnson Space Center (NASA-JSC); 10R, NASA Johnson Space Center (NASA-JSC); 11T, © Bettmann/Corbis; 11BL, NASA Johnson Space Center (NASA-JSC); 11BR, © NASA/Space Frontiers/Getty Images/Newscom.com; 12, © Cynthia Johnson//Time Life Pictures/Getty Images; 13, NASA Johnson Space Center (NASA-JSC); 15, © Space Frontiers/Hulton Archive/Getty Images; 16, NASA Johnson Space Center (NASA-JSC); 17, NASA Johnson Space Center (NASA-JSC); 18, NASA Johnson Space Center (NASA-JSC); 19, NASA Johnson Space Center (NASA-JSC); 20, © MPI/Getty Images; 21, NASA Johnson Space Center (NASA-JSC); 22, NASA Johnson Space Center (NASA-JSC); 23, NASA Johnson Space Center (NASA-JSC); 24, NASA Johnson Space Center (NASA-JSC); 25, Courtesy Ronald Reagan Library; 26, NASA Johnson Space Center (NASA-JSC); 27, NASA Johnson Space Center (NASA-JSC); 28T, NASA Johnson Space Center (NASA-JSC); 28B, NASA Johnson Space Center (NASA-JSC); 29T, NASA Johnson Space Center (NASA-JSC); 29B, NASA Johnson Space Center (NASA-JSC); 29 Background, NASA Johnson Space Center (NASA-JSC).

Publisher: Kenn Goin
Project Editor: Lisa Wiseman
Creative Director: Spencer Brinker
Design: Dawn Beard Creative
Photo Researcher: Marty Levick

Library of Congress Cataloging-in-Publication Data

Caper, William.
The Challenger Space Shuttle explosion / by William Caper.
    p. cm. — (Code red)
Includes bibliographical references and index.
ISBN-13: 978-1-59716-367-5 (library binding)
ISBN-10: 1-59716-367-8 (library binding)
1. Challenger (Spacecraft)—Accidents—Juvenile literature. 2. Space vehicle accidents—United States—Juvenile literature. I. Title.

TL867.C36 2007
363.12'465—dc22

2006030257

For more information, write to Bearport Publishing Company, Inc., 101 Fifth Avenue, Suite 6R, New York, New York 10003. Printed in the United States of America.

10 9 8 7 6 5 4 3 2 1

Contents

Ready to Launch

It was the morning of January 28, 1986. The space **shuttle** *Challenger* stood on the launch pad at the Kennedy Space Center in Florida. The day was very cold. Despite the weather, a large crowd had gathered to see the launch.

Challenger's crew walked to the launch pad on the morning of January 28, 1986.

The launch of *Challenger* had been delayed six times due to equipment problems and powerful winds.

The commander of the shuttle was Francis "Dick" Scobee. He spoke to the **NASA** control center by radio.

"Two minutes," Scobee said. *Challenger* was about to liftoff.

As the countdown continued, the seven crew members aboard *Challenger* joked with one another. So far, things were going well. However, in just a few minutes, that would all change.

A large crowd gathered to watch the liftoff.

The Space Age Begins

The **Space Age** began in 1957 when the Soviet Union sent a **satellite** into space. Four years later, the first **astronauts** traveled in **capsules** carried on powerful rockets. These capsules took people into **orbit** around Earth. However, they could be used only once. When the capsules returned to Earth, they splashed down into the ocean.

America's early space travelers flew in Mercury capsules like this one.

In 1972, NASA began developing a better way to carry people into space. Workers designed a new spacecraft called the shuttle. Unlike the capsules, the shuttle could glide back to Earth and land on a runway. Then it could be used again for another **mission**.

Astronaut John Glenn was the first American to orbit Earth in a Mercury capsule.

The first shuttle was named *Enterprise*, after the spaceship on the TV show *Star Trek*.

The Space Shuttle

Between 1979 and 1985, NASA built four shuttles. Each one was named after a famous sailing ship—*Columbia*, *Atlantis*, *Discovery*, and *Challenger*. By 1986, the four shuttles had made a total of 24 trips to space.

The first shuttle to fly into space was *Columbia* in 1981. It landed at Edwards Air Force Base in California.

❝ Every mission that anybody gets is very demanding, challenging, and exciting. ❞
—Judith A. Resnik, astronaut, talking about shuttle flights

From the beginning, shuttle crews tried to learn more about space. For example, on *Columbia*'s trip in 1981, the shuttle carried equipment to measure Earth's **atmosphere**. On other missions, astronauts observed Earth, the sun, and the stars.

Sometimes shuttle crews did science experiments in their special space lab. They studied what happened to plants, animals, and the human body in space.

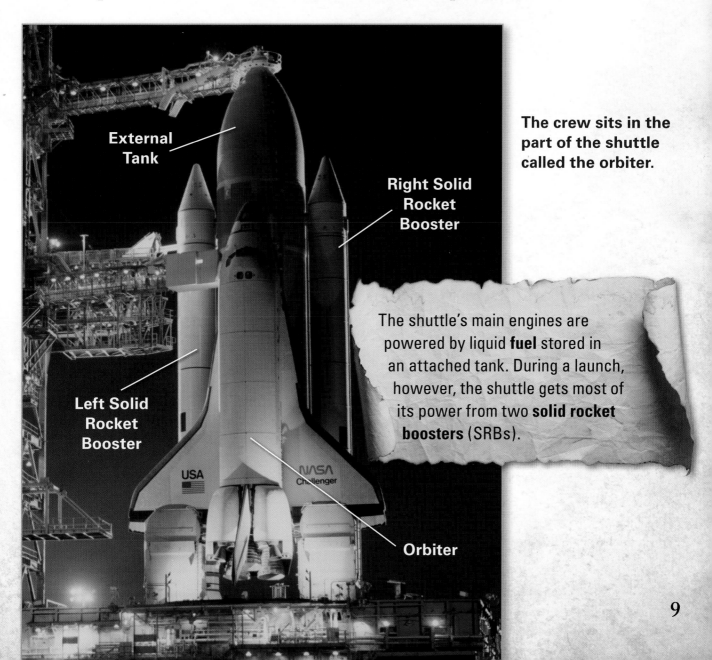

External Tank

Right Solid Rocket Booster

The crew sits in the part of the shuttle called the orbiter.

The shuttle's main engines are powered by liquid **fuel** stored in an attached tank. During a launch, however, the shuttle gets most of its power from two **solid rocket boosters** (SRBs).

Left Solid Rocket Booster

USA

NASA Challenger

Orbiter

Challenger's Crew

The 1986 *Challenger* flight had seven crew members. Dick Scobee was the commander. This was his second spaceflight. The pilot, Michael J. Smith, was on his first mission in space.

Along with Scobee and Smith, there were three mission **specialists** on board: Ellison S. Onizuka, Ronald E. McNair, and Judith A. Resnik. Each of them had flown on a shuttle mission before.

By the time he flew on *Challenger*, Ellison Onizuka had already spent 74 hours in space.

Dick Scobee eats a meal during a mission in 1984.

During his career as a pilot, Michael Smith flew 28 different kinds of aircraft.

There were also two crew members who were not astronauts. Gregory B. Jarvis worked for a company that built airplanes. His job was to gather information to help design better fuel tanks for different spacecraft. Christa McAuliffe was a teacher.

Judith Resnik (left) and Christa McAuliffe (right) meet with the media after a countdown dress rehearsal.

Gregory Jarvis was supposed to be on an earlier shuttle mission. However, crew assignment changes put him on the 1986 *Challenger* flight.

Ronald McNair plays the saxophone during a 1984 mission.

A Teacher in Space

Having McAuliffe on board made this shuttle mission special. In 1984, NASA had started a new program. It would allow people who were not astronauts to travel to space. President Ronald Reagan announced that the first person in the program would be a teacher.

More than 11,000 teachers from across the country applied. The judges asked their top choices many questions. At last, they chose a winner—Christa McAuliffe.

McAuliffe talking to the press after it was announced that she would be the first teacher in space

Christa McAuliffe mailed her application for NASA's Teacher in Space program on the last possible day—February 1, 1985.

McAuliffe taught social studies in New Hampshire. Now, after several months of NASA training, she would teach from space. Students all over the country would be able to watch her on television.

During training, McAuliffe experienced being weightless.

"I think it's going to be very exciting for kids to be able to turn on the TV and see the teacher teaching from space."
–Christa McAuliffe

Challenger's Mission

During *Challenger*'s seven-day mission, McAuliffe planned to teach two lessons from space. Her first would be a tour of the shuttle. The second would be about the future of space travel.

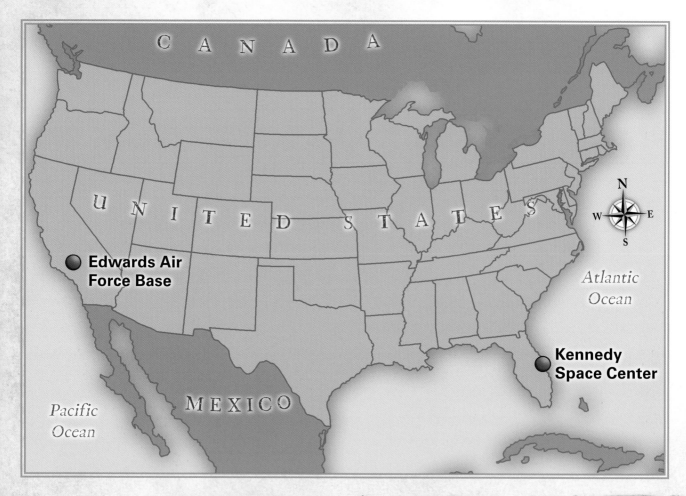

Challenger was launched from Kennedy Space Center in Florida. It was scheduled to land back there or at Edwards Air Force Base in California.

The 1986 *Challenger* flight was mission number STS-51L. *STS* stands for Space Transportation System, and 51L refers to the exact mission.

Ellison Onizuka had special plans, too. This mission was a rare chance for him to study Halley's **Comet**. The comet's orbit brings it near Earth only once every 76 years.

The other crew members would be busy as well. They were going to use the shuttle's robot arm to set up a new satellite. They also planned to do science experiments in space.

As Halley's Comet approaches the sun, it is followed by a trail of dust and ice called the tail.

Decision to Launch

The night before the launch, worried **engineers** met with NASA officials. They discussed delaying the liftoff due to cold weather.

The engineers feared the cold might damage rubber seals on the shuttle's SRBs. These seals kept the SRBs' **joints** tightly closed. If the joints came open, hot gases could escape and damage the shuttle.

The night before liftoff, icicles formed on the launch tower. The ice melted by the time of the launch.

Since the launch had already been delayed due to weather, NASA officials did not want to **postpone** it again. The engineers could not prove for sure that the shuttle would not be safe. By the end of the meeting, they agreed the launch would go as planned the next day.

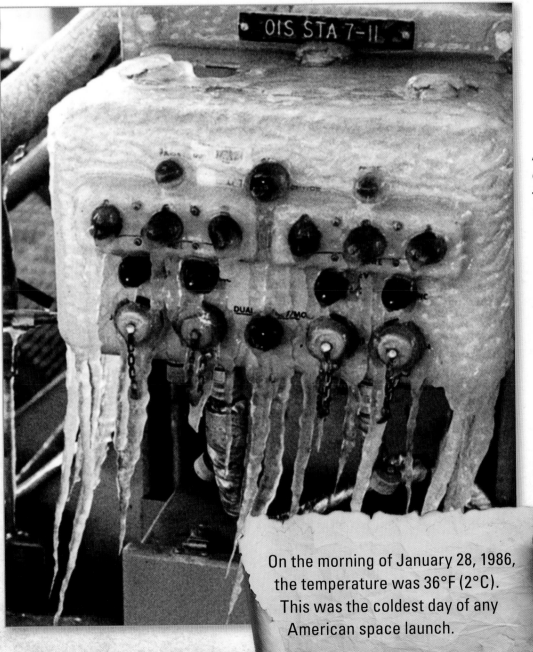

A machine on the launch tower covered in ice

On the morning of January 28, 1986, the temperature was 36°F (2°C). This was the coldest day of any American space launch.

Here We Go

In the morning, the crew members waited inside *Challenger*, ready to begin their mission. As the clock ticked down, a piece of equipment moved into place for liftoff. Onizuka made a joke.

"Doesn't it go the other way?" he asked. Everyone laughed.

"Everybody strap in tight. We're about to go for the ride of our lives."

—*Challenger* commander Dick Scobee, talking to the crew before liftoff

As the launch approached, the crew's excitement grew. At six seconds before liftoff, the shuttle's powerful main engines **ignited** with a roar.

"There they go," Scobee announced.

"Aaall riiight!" exclaimed Resnik.

Challenger began to inch upward.

"Here we go," said Smith.

Part of the astronauts' training included practicing what it would be like on the shuttle before liftoff.

Challenger had more than 2,000 instruments and displays. The shuttle also carried five computers.

Liftoff

At 11:38 A.M., *Challenger* thundered off the ground. A cloud of steam rose next to it. Flames shot from the bottom of the shuttle. Its ground-shaking roar knocked books off shelves in a nearby trailer.

Challenger soared into the air. People shaded their eyes as they followed the shuttle into the sunny sky.

Challenger lifting off from the launch pad

Suddenly, everything changed. A bright ball of fire flashed in the sky. Thick clouds of white smoke appeared. People stared. What was going on?

At **mission control** in Houston, Texas, NASA officials knew *Challenger* was in trouble. Their computers were no longer receiving information from the shuttle.

"We have a report . . . that the vehicle has exploded."

–Steven Nesbitt, mission control observer in Houston

The space shuttle exploded into a giant fireball 73 seconds after liftoff.

What Happened?

What went wrong? It turned out the engineers' fears came true. The extreme cold had caused one rubber seal to shrink. This **O-ring** became too small to close its joint properly. Hot gases escaped during liftoff, damaging one SRB and the fuel tank.

As the shuttle shot higher into the sky, the broken parts twisted loose. They banged together, causing even more damage. Dangerous gases began pouring out with great force.

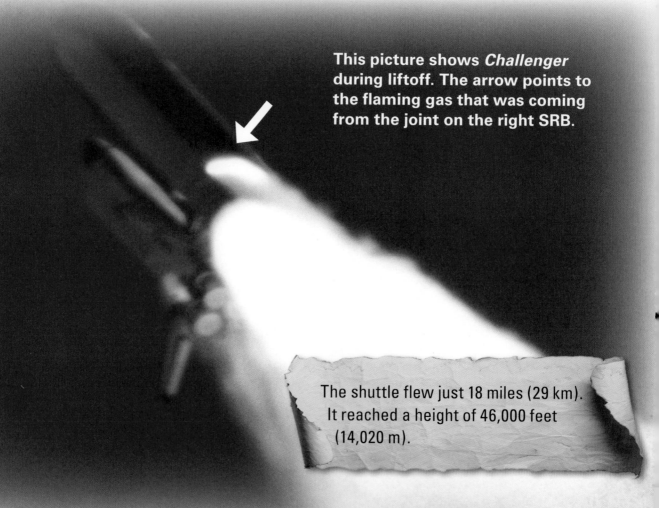

This picture shows *Challenger* during liftoff. The arrow points to the flaming gas that was coming from the joint on the right SRB.

The shuttle flew just 18 miles (29 km). It reached a height of 46,000 feet (14,020 m).

The shuttle could not stand the extra force. The fuel tank broke apart, along with *Challenger*. Its pieces crashed down to Earth. No one on board survived.

After the disaster, U.S. Coast Guard and Navy ships picked up pieces from the wrecked shuttle in the Atlantic Ocean. This piece of debris is from the left SRB.

" If we are very, very careful, we can still have an outstanding space shuttle program."

–John Young, astronaut, talking about preventing future shuttle accidents

A Nation in Shock

The sad news spread quickly. Pictures of the disaster were shown again and again on television. The loss of *Challenger* stunned people across the United States and the world.

Many students around the country had been watching the launch. Brandyn Siegler, age nine, saw the accident on television. His whole school had been watching. "We all cried—students, teachers," he remembered.

The NASA flight directors study data in the flight control room. The disaster can be seen on the screen in the back of the picture.

That evening, President Reagan spoke to the nation, especially to American schoolchildren. In his speech, the president said, "It's hard to understand, but sometimes painful things like this happen. It's all part of the process of exploration and discovery."

President Reagan spoke to the nation from the Oval Office in Washington, D.C., on the evening of January 28, 1986.

A special **commission** investigated the disaster. Two of its members were Neil Armstrong, the first man to walk on the moon, and Sally Ride, the first American woman in space.

Flying into the Future

After the tragedy, NASA made many changes. The O-rings and SRB joints on the remaining shuttles were **redesigned**.

NASA also put new safety checks in place. In the future, officials would postpone a launch if there were any concerns at all about safety.

The exploration of space continues today. This picture shows an astronaut on a space walk during a 2006 mission on the shuttle *Discovery*.

There will always be some risk in exploring space. After *Challenger* was lost, President Reagan said, "The future . . . belongs to the brave." He was speaking partly about the courageous people who flew the shuttle. He was also speaking about all those who will journey into space in the future.

Today, shuttles often transport people and equipment to the International Space Station.

In 1991, a new shuttle, *Endeavour*, was built to replace *Challenger*. Its first flight took place in 1992.

" There will be more shuttle flights and . . . more teachers in space. Nothing ends here; our hopes and our journeys continue. **"**

–President Ronald Reagan, in his speech to the nation, January 28, 1986

Many people played important roles in the events connected to the *Challenger* disaster. Here are four of them.

Francis "Dick" Scobee **was the commander of *Challenger*'s 1986 mission.**

- Learned to fly in the Air Force
- Served as a test pilot, flying more than 45 different kinds of aircraft
- Was the pilot on *Challenger*'s fifth space flight, in 1984
- During the 1984 mission, helped retrieve and repair a satellite that was in orbit

Judith A. Resnik **was a mission specialist on *Challenger*.**

- In 1984, became the second American woman in space
- Liked to be called by her initials, J.R.
- Helped set up three satellites and conduct medical research on the shuttle *Discovery*'s first flight, in 1984

Ronald E. McNair **was a mission specialist on** *Challenger.*

- Was a fifth-degree black belt karate teacher
- Was one of the first three African American astronauts chosen by NASA
- On his first space mission, operated the shuttle's robot arm, moving objects in space

Christa McAuliffe **was a payload specialist on** *Challenger.*

- Had many interests, including tennis, volleyball, and running
- Taught high school social studies and was supposed to be the first teacher in space
- Was popular with reporters and brought attention to the Teacher in Space program

Glossary

astronauts (ASS-truh-*nawts*) people who travel into space

atmosphere (AT-muhss-fihr) gases that surround a planet

capsules (KAP-suhlz) small compartments or vehicles, often used in space travel

comet (KOM-it) a small icy body that travels through space and develops a tail as it moves closer to the sun

commission (kuh-MISH-uhn) a group of people directed to solve a problem

engineers (*en*-juh-NIHRZ) people who are trained to work with technology such as machines, engines, or chemicals

fuel (FYOO-uhl) something that is burned to produce heat or power

ignited (ig-NITE-id) heated up or caused fuel to burn

joints (JOINTS) places where two parts meet or come together

mission (MISH-uhn) certain jobs or tasks to be performed in space

mission control (MISH-uhn kuhn-TROHL) the command center on Earth where people can track a spacecraft with the help of computers

NASA (NA-suh) the National Aeronautics and Space Administration; the government agency in charge of the U.S. space program

orbit (OR-bit) path of an object as it circles a planet or sun

O-ring (*oh*-RING) a rubber object used to seal a joint on a spacecraft

postpone (pohst-PONE) to put off until a later time

redesigned (ree-di-ZINED) changed what something looks like, or is used for

satellite (SAT-uh-*lite*) a spacecraft placed in orbit that is able to send signals back to Earth

shuttle (SHUHT-uhl) a vehicle that travels back and forth over a set route

solid rocket boosters (SOL-id ROK-it BOO-sturz) large white rockets that hold fuel and help launch the space shuttle into orbit

Space Age (SPAYSS AJE) the time in history when people started exploring space

specialists (SPESH-uh-lists) people with a great deal of training in a particular job, task, or field of learning

Bibliography

Harland, David M. *The Story of the Space Shuttle.* New York: Springer Praxis Books (2004).

Yenne, Bill. *The Encyclopedia of US Spacecraft.* New York: Exeter Books (1985).

www.hq.nasa.gov/office/pao/History/sts51l.html

Read More

Bernstein, Joanne E., and Rose Blue. *Judith Resnik:* Challenger *Astronaut.* New York: Dutton Children's Books (1990).

Bredeson, Carmen. *The* Challenger *Disaster: Tragic Space Flight.* Springfield, NJ: Enslow Publishers (1999).

Jeffrey, Laura S. *Christa McAuliffe: A Space Biography.* Springfield, NJ: Enslow Publishers (1998).

McNeese, Tim. *The* Challenger *Disaster.* Danbury, CT: Children's Press (2003).

Learn More Online

To learn more about the *Challenger* disaster, visit **www.bearportpublishing.com/CodeRed**

Index

About the Author

William Caper has written books about history, science, film, and many other topics. He lives in San Francisco, with his wife, Erin, and their dog, Face.